Haunted Nottinghamshire Vol. 2

by
Len Moakes

ISBN 0 946404 72 0

With a forword by Tom Perrott
Chairman of the Ghost Club.

Printed & Published by
Footprint Press Ltd.,
"From footprint to finished book."
19, Moseley Street,
Ripley,
Derbyshire.
DE5 3DA

Ghost and Legends Series.

The Supernatural is The Natural Not Yet Understood
Elbert Hubbard, The Note Book (1927)

FOREWORD

by Tom Perrott

It was with a feeling of great pleasure that I accepted the author's kind invitation to write a Foreword to this, his second book on Haunted Nottinghamshire. Nottingham is a city that I have always regarded with great affection as I not only happened to be stationed there during the last war when hostilities ceased in Europe, but I also had the good fortune to meet there my then wife-to-be.

When Len Moakes placed the city fairly and squarely on the 'spectral map' in his first book I really felt that in the ghostly sense the city 'had arrived', and that many of its psychic secrets were being revealed for the first time, as to the best of my knowledge, this side of its varied life had never previously been recorded in detail. The author has again rectified this omission by producing another delightful collection of accounts of local hauntings which one feels have been at least accurately researched and have not just been manufactured and embellished for the spectral delectation and the psychic titillation of any tourist who might be visiting the area.

The study of local hauntings is a fascinating one and there are two ways in which it may be approached. Firstly through the eyes of the Folklorist and secondly through the dispassionate investigation of the genuine Psychical Researcher, or in vulgar modern parlance the 'Ghostbuster.' The Folklorist is not concerned with proving the veracity of ghost stories. His task is to record them before details, often never having been put on paper, become lost and forgotten through the passing of time or as a result of the demise of the persons who often retained them as childhood memories. The psychical researcher, when reports of allegedly inexplicable happenings are brought to his notice, will, if it is practicable, duly investigate them and endeavour to find a rational explanation for them.

I feel that in this informative volume Len skilfully combines the best of two psychic worlds in that not only has he interviewed many of the witnesses concerned for the accounts of their experiences, but he has also carried out many painstaking 'on-the-spot' investigations with members of his group. After reading this book one gains the impression that the author does not depend upon the works of others to chronicle the many strange events that he so eloquently describes, and one cannot help but feel that he really has involved himself with his characters and has personally visited many of the sites in Nottinghamshire which had so many hitherto unrecorded ghost stories to tell.

Tom Perrott
Chairman of The Ghost Club

3

INTRODUCTION

In this age of advanced technology one would have thought that ghosts had no place in today's world. Yet books and magazine articles continue to be written about them, television, film and radio programmes are produced about them, and they are brought to our attention by the Press at every opportunity. For ghosts continue to enthrall, fascinate and frighten us today as they did our distant forebears and since the beginning of recorded history.

Opinion as to what a ghost is remains divided. Those who subscribe to spiritualism maintain, for the most part, that a ghost is a restless spirit which is unable to cross the 'great divide' and remains 'earthbound.' The psychical researcher, whilst trying to keep an open mind and remaining impartial, considers that a ghost is, in its simplest form, a possible playback of past events or happenings which have somehow become etched onto the atmosphere of the present. For example, there are accounts of battles being re-enacted (both visual and auditory) reports of phantom ships, cars, buses, trains, aircraft and even buildings. This of course, raises the question — how can man made objects possess a spirit? Perhaps one day research will prove that the word 'ghost' needs to be re-defined.

That ghosts do exist, however, (though not necessarily constituting proof of survival after death) there is little doubt and, contrary to popular belief, they do not confine their attentions to historic houses and isolated churchyards. They are likely to be encountered in a modest semi-detached house and in even recently constructed buildings. A few years ago the staff at a newly built supermarket in Nottingham which was built on the site of a disused graveyard (and possibly because of their collective knowledge of this) experienced a number of seemingly inexplicable happenings which ceased after a visit by a local clergyman and his subsequent blessing — not exorcism — of the premises. To date, as far as I am aware, this seems to have been successful but this may be due, at least in part, to the fact that the staff were aware that something positive was being done on their behalf to allay the problem.

My interest and research into this fascinating but nebulous and often contradictory subject has brought me into contact with some delightful and interesting people, thus resulting in some firm friendships. It has also, unfortunately, proved that the paranormal is the province of some unscrupulous individuals and self-styled experts. I advise the reader not to pay for someone to rid them of a supposed ghost. Genuine psychical researchers do not levy a fee for their services.

Together with other members of the Nottingham Psychical Research Group I have conducted many investigations in reputedly haunted properties in Nottinghamshire and the neighbouring counties and have studied numerous authoritative publications about the paranormal. Whilst this makes us knowledgeable about the subject it does not, we feel, entitle us to term ourselves 'experts.' People have contacted us in the hope that we can rid them of their ghost. This we are unable to do and our investigations of these domestic hauntings have no place in this book. We can, however, try to determine whether a property is haunted and if after an investigation we consider that it is, suggest that the occupants contact a clergyman of a recognised denomination and not a commercial 'medium' who may only exacerbate the problem.

It must be remembered, however, that many prosaic happenings, especially during the hours of darkness, can be genuinely thought and mistaken to be paranormal. In old houses airlocks in antiquated plumbing can produce unnerving noises, whilst floor boards expanding or contracting can, together with echoes from an adjoining house, be easily mistaken for disembodied footsteps. A not uncommon occurrence are air traps. When a door is opened in one part of a house, others may open or close owing to suction or compression and strange lights may simply be due to the reflection cast by the headlights of passing vehicles. These are but a few of the many factors that the psychical researcher will look for and take into account before considering the paranormal — but the percipients can always be assured of a sympathetic ear.

Following the publication of 'Haunted Nottinghamshire' in 1987, many people of all ages and callings have contacted me to inform me of their own encounters with the paranormal. Some of these are recorded in this book. Readers will not find fabricated stories but a selection of serious and unembellished accounts of eerie and mysterious happenings which have occurred, and still occur from time to time, not only at some of the county's historic houses, but also at its more modest edifices.

All the accounts recorded here were written in good faith, and whilst some of my informants have insisted that I preserve their anonymity, others have not objected to my inclusion of their name in the text.

Surveys have revealed that approximately one person in every ten may, at sometime during their lifetime, encounter a ghost. Needless to say, should any readers of this book happen to be amongst that number I would be delighted to hear from them. Despite the evidence which suggests that ghosts do exist there will always be sceptics. Might I ask these to remember that many people were, prior to their own experience, sceptics too. As I myself was.

The Nottingham Psychical Research Group wish it to be known that it has no connection or affiliation with any group or organisation with similar title or any person or persons advertising as 'psychical researchers' or 'consultants' who, by inference, might use the reputation of the Nottingham Psychical Research Group to further their aims.

ANNESLEY HALL

Annesley Hall, the former home of one of Nottingham-shire's oldest families, the Chaworth-Musters, is steeped in history and romance. Here, where deer from the surrounding park once wandered over the lawns, Byron courted his boyhood love, Mary Ann Chaworth. Today this mellow house is little more than a shell, but although its furnishings and rich panelling are gone it still retains its dignity and an atmosphere of times past; and also it seems, its phantoms.

When the Quaker poet William Howitt visited Annesley Hall in 1840 he was told that it was haunted by two ghosts. One was that of a lady who was said to rise from a well in the grounds, the other being that of a woman who had died in childbirth. Down the years there have been many rumours of ghosts seen in the vicinity of the house.

Since its formation in 1982 the Nottingham Psychical Research Group has spent numerous all night vigils in both the house and grounds in order to investigate these, usually without incident. But during an investigation in 1983 three members of the group and a guest 'medium' witnessed at 12.45am a luminescent shape, resembling a woman, drift over the lawn and for which an explanation could not be found. This was recorded in some detail in **Haunted Nottinghamshire.** Shortly after its publication my friend and Chairman of The Ghost Club,   Tom Perrott, sent me a copy of an article written by Mr. Bert Ashworth, M.B.E. dated 14th October 1984 and to whom I am grateful for allowing me to quote from this.

One night some twenty years earlier Mr. Ashworth was motoring from Eastwood en-route to Mansfield when, as he approached the high wall which shields Annesley Hall from the gaze of curious motorists he 'suddenly became concious of a distinct clammy feeling — a cold sweat, and on reaching the first curve in the road saw a tall lady-like figure wearing a large ornate hat and a long white dress — and then the lights of an approaching car shone directly onto the figure which then hurried to the side of the road and seemed to vanish into the wall.' He slowed down but did not stop and the clammy feeling remained with him for the remainder of his journey. Arriving home he gave an account of his experience to his wife and son. For some months following his son would ask, 'Seen any ghosts lately Dad?' Several months later however his son became friendly with a young lady whose parents' home backed onto the grounds of Newstead Abbey. It transpired that her father had also seen a ghostly lady in white in the Abbey grounds.

I recently received a telephone call from a Mrs. Wanda Blanchard of North Muskham near Newark. During a subsequent interview she told me of an experience that she had suffered when driving past Annesley Hall one November night in 1970 when on her way to Harlow Wood Hospital where she worked as a physiotherapist. Over two decades later her memory of that experience is still vivid. "As I approached the Hall I saw, on the right hand side of the road what appeared to be a woman who began to cross the road — it all happened very quickly — but I swerved the car to the right, towards the wall, to avoid colliding with this person. I could not avoid her. She came right up to the windscreen and

8

I drove right through her. I then realised that it wasn't a woman but a figure wearing a dense black cowl which I had taken to be a headscarf. The figure then disappeared. I was so shocked at not feeling the expected bump and by driving through the figure that I kept on driving. I was in a state of shock. It was a long time before I drove past Annesley Hall again, but when I eventually did go past I noticed a doorway in the high wall and it was a short distance beyond there, where the road dips, where the incident happened.'

Adjacent to Annesley Hall is the forlorn decaying ruin of All Saints' Church which had an aisle built as a chantry chapel and was known as Felly Chapel after a small priory some two miles away. Founded in the 12th century, one of five Augustinian houses in the county, this priory was the home of The Black Canons. They wore black cassocks and cloaks.

During the 14th century this corner of Nottinghamshire saw the ravages of the bubonic plague and some of its victims, including the monks of Felly Priory who tended them and became victims themselves, were interred beneath the now moss encrusted paving of All Saints' Church. Had Mrs. Blanchard, that night in 1970, encountered the shade of one of the victims of the 'Black Death?' Perhaps one night, as you drive by Annesley Hall, you might also chance to witness one of its phantoms.

Many historic houses have a secret passage or tunnel. These were used as escape routes in times of political instability or to conceal fugitives. It has long been rumoured that such a tunnel exists at Annesley Hall. In 1988, when the cellars of the house were undergoing renovation, an entrance was discovered. Although it was blocked by rubble the subsequent examination revealed two steps descending, thus perhaps indicating that there may be some truth in this rumour.

ANNESLEY HALL REVISITED

In October 1989 I was interviewed inside Annesley Hall by Mark Cummings for a BBC Radio Nottingham feature about the county's ghosts. I described how, some two years previously, a member of the Nottingham Psychical Research Group experienced a perplexing incident at the house.

Ghosts have not, as far as I am aware, been witnessed inside Annesley Hall although people have claimed to have sensed something 'watching' them and of 'hearing doors slam.' At the time of writing Annesley Hall is owned by Mr. Dennis Rye, a property developer. With his kind permission Adrian Pearce-Naylor, myself and a member of the group I will call Paul, were able to spend the night of 7th November 1987 inside the house.

Adrian and I arrived at 10.00pm to be presented with the keys by Mr. Jonathan Rye. Shortly after his departure Adrian and I made a preliminary examination of the house then visited the nearby churchyard. Here stands a memorial dedicated to several members of the Chaworth-Musters family. At 11.00pm we returned to the house to meet Paul and proceeded to place our equipment in various rooms.

At 4.20am we ascended a flight of stairs and on reaching the landing, both Adrian and Paul commented on the strange atmosphere and the sudden coldness in this area. It was agreed that the coldness may have been due to the staircase causing an updraught of air. We decided, however, to spend 30 minutes in this area, in darkness and silence, in order to see if anyone received impressions of anything unusual. At the end of this corridor was a room which afforded us the best view of the corridor and landing. We positioned ourselves there and sat facing the corridor. After some minutes Adrian indicated that he could see something. From behind his chair we saw what appeared to be a shadow which moved slowly from the head of the stairs and crossed to the right of the corridor. However, at the end of the corridor was a window.

The moon was out and the shadow, we felt, was caused by a cloud passing in front of the moon.

After the 30 minutes had elapsed we changed places and resumed our experiment, this time with Paul facing the window. Some 20 minutes later he indicated that he could see something. Adrian and I stood behind him and again saw a shadow. Paul was amazed by our lack of reaction and told us that he could clearly see a young boy with fair hair, wearing a white shirt with a frilled collar and dark trousers. Adrian and I continued to see only a shadow. Paul went on to say that the boy had been joined by a young girl. She was attired in a long grey dress. He told us that the names John and Mary were being conveyed to him and he felt that our presence was unwelcome. The figures, and the shadow, then faded away.

It is interesting to postulate a possible explanation for this incident. Paul is in no doubt about what he saw and he has given me a signed statement to this effect. However, as this was only his second investigation at a reputedly haunted house it is quite possible that his experience was subjective. But, in the churchyard is the memorial to the Chaworth-Musters family. He was unaware of this. It bears the names of a brother and sister, John and Mary Anne. The dates of their deaths, however, from which we can determine their ages when they died, reveal that they had no comparability with the youthful figures which he had witnessed.

When I told Paul about the memorial, and the names it bears, he was disbelieving and asked for proof of its existence. A visit to the churchyard gave him this. He decided to leave. Was Paul's experience subjective? Or did he manifest a latent psychic ability of which he was previously unaware and which had enabled him to witness a possible playback of past events?

NEWSTEAD ABBEY

Newstead Abbey is, without doubt, the county's best known historic haunted house. Founded in 1170 by Henry II for a community of Augustinian Canons in expiation for the murder of Thomas à Becket, it was purchased by Sir John Byron of Colwick in 1540. He extended the property which, in 1798, was inherited by eleven year old George Gordon Noel Byron. This 6th Lord Byron became one of Nottinghamshire's most famous sons and literary figures. Through the centuries the Abbey and its grounds have been the scene of numerous inexplicable happenings and encounters with phantoms.

In 1817 Byron, unable to maintain his inheritance, sold the house to a Colonel Wildman. Late one night the Colonel was awakened by the sound of a heavy garden roller being pushed along the gravel path beneath his window. There was nothing to be seen. In the morning he questioned the gardener who insisted that the roller was always secured by chains after dark. Some years later when Lady Elizabeth Stanhope was a guest of the Wildman family her daughter rushed into her room claiming that someone was pushing a garden roller beneath her window. The subsequent examination, by daylight, revealed that the roller was, as on the previous occasion, securely chained.

Newstead Abbey's most well known phantoms are those of the White Lady, thought to be the wraith of the enigmatic Sophia Hyatt whose remains lie in Hucknall churchyard, and the Black Friar, a brother of the old monastery. Testimony reveals that these phantoms are still to be encountered by those abroad in the Abbey grounds after dark.

In the first volume of **Haunted Nottinghamshire** I wrote of a doctor who, some years ago, supposedly met the Black Friar. As I was unable to discover his identity, or when this encounter occurred, I said that we must consider this story to be apocryphal. Soon after its publication I received a telephone call from a Mr. Andrew Congdon, a local barrister who confirmed that this story was true.

Mr. Congdon and his wife had once lived at a house in the Abbey grounds. One night in December 1962 when ice and snow lay thick upon the ground and the area was shrouded by dense fog, Mrs. Congdon went into labour. Mr. Congdon telephoned for a doctor. Doctor Phillip Rutter had been to their home socially several times previously but, owing to the fog, on this occasion he became lost. He stopped his car to enquire for directions from a figure which close observation revealed to be that of a monk. It ignored his enquiry and disappeared into the fog. The encounter occurred between 11.00pm and 12.00pm.

Not only am I grateful to Mr. Congdon for taking the time to substantiate this story but also for pointing out that I had made an error. Doctor Rutter had encountered the Black Friar somewhere in the vicinity of the small bridge by the waterfall in the Abbey grounds and not, as I had originally been told and recorded, by the Abbey's main gates. Doctor Rutter now lives in Canada. ·

Until recently, a Mr. Kenyon Adlington Barrett, a publican from Kirkby-in-Ashfield would, most Saturday afternoons, take his two sons then aged three and five years old, to Newstead Abbey to fish in its lake. Because of the youngsters enthusiasm for their sport they would not begin to pack their fishing tackle away until the approach of dusk. One Autumn evening as they were preparing to leave, their chosen spot was, owing to the overhanging trees and encroaching shrubbery, already in deep shadow. The path between the bushes and the lake was narrow. They left in single file, the youngest son in front with his father walking behind him to ensure that he did not fall into the lake, with the eldest son bringing up the rear. The elder son was, as usual, enthusing over the days sport but the younger one was unusually silent. His father attributed this to his being tired. During the journey home he remained uncommunicative. That evening as his father was putting him to bed the boy enquired "Daddy, who was that man in the black hood who was watching us as we were leaving." Mr. Adlington Barrett suddenly became cold for he knew of the stories of the Black Friar. Is it likely that a three year old boy might?

The waterfall in the grounds of Newstead Abbey appears to be, depending upon one's point of view, a propitious spot in which to encounter phantoms. Not only that of the Black Friar but also, it would seem, of the White Lady. A retired taxi driver, a Mr. O. J. Walker, told me of his never to be forgotten experience when driving past in 1975.

Shortly before midnight, after taking a fare into the grounds, he became aware that as he approached the waterfall the temperature inside his car had dropped and he became extremely cold. He happened to glance in his rear view mirror and was astounded to see, sitting in the back of his car, a figure which sat staring straight ahead, attired in white and 'wearing a sort of head-dress.' 'Its features were vague and some yards beyond the waterfall it suddenly disappeared when the temperature inside the car returned to normal.' As this gentleman described the figure's features as being vague I enquired whether he had gained an impression of it being male or female. He replied, "Definitely female."

An interesting story, which, had it not been for my informant's obvious sincerity, I would not have countenanced including here.

In Mr. Ashworth's account of his experience at Annesley Hall he refers to a gentleman whose house adjoined the grounds of Newstead Abbey and who had witnessed a 'ghost-like lady in white' there. Might this have been that same figure?

A CHAIR AND ITS PHANTOM

There are numerous stories about items of furniture which appear to be haunted, from clocks which seem to have a prescience of death, to rocking chairs which move without the aid of human agency. In her book **Haunted East Anglia,** Joan Forman includes an account about an antique chair which, at the time of her writing, was owned by a Mr. Bryan Hall of Banningham Rectory, Norfolk. Its previous owner, a Mrs. Mary Hutt, was the widow of Canon H. R. M. Hutt who had been a Rector of Bingham, near Nottingham.

Following the death of her husband Mrs. Hutt moved to Dilham in Norfolk where Mr. Hall's father was the vicar and where Mr. Hall met her and first saw the chair. He made some remark about it and she told him that she had purchased it shortly after the First World War from an antique shop in Nottingham when she and her husband were living in Bingham. Mrs. Hutt related to him how, during a thunderstorm, she had taken shelter in the doorway of the shop and had heard a voice crying 'Save me! 'Save me! Looking into the shop she saw a chair in which sat a red-haired woman wearing a 'sumptuous dress' and, to her mind, an expression indicating a violent temper. She entered the shop and the woman repeated her entreaty. Mrs. Hutt, uncertain as to what she should do, was then joined by the proprietor and she nervously told him that she had come in only to shelter from the rain. Turning back to the chair she found that the woman had gone. Feeling obligated to purchase something she chose the chair and was informed that it had come from Newstead Abbey.

The chair was transferred from the shop to her car but

during the journey home her chauffeur experienced some difficulty with the steering although there had been no such problem on the journey into Nottingham. Arriving home the chair was placed overnight in the servants' hall and one of the maids was instructed to scrub it with soap and water in the morning. After breakfast the maid told Mrs. Hutt that she had been unable to do this and that she thought the chair to be 'bewitched!' Mrs. Hutt agreed to wash it herself.

What occurred at this juncture, Mr. Hall was unable to tell Joan Forman in detail — save that whenever the chair was placed by a fireplace, whether the fire was alight or not — the red haired woman would be seen seated in it and it was decided that if the household were to have peace then the chair would have to be kept away from fireplaces.

Mrs Hutt eventually moved to a rented house in Norfolk and the first day after moving in her dog became excited and ran to the window and began to bark. She paused in what she was doing to try to find the cause of her pets agitation and looked out of the window to see, coming up the drive, the red-haired woman. Her search for the chair revealed it to be standing by a fireplace where it had been left by the removal men. She was not surprised when the phantom entered the room and sat on it.

When Mrs. Hutt died she left the chair to Mr. Hall on the condition that he must not experiment with it by placing it by a fireplace. He was pleased to have the chair and to honour her wishes. On learning that it had been left to him Mr. Hall arranged for its delivery by the village postmaster. When it was placed in his car he experienced steering difficulties en-route to Mr. Hall's home. Joan Forman speculated about the identity of the phantom red-haired woman, the chair's associations with Newstead Abbey and about fire, the catalyst to the phantom's appearance. Might there once have been a blaze at the house and was the phantom that of a member of the household who had died there as a result of this? She made enquiries from a friend who had been brought up in the village of Newstead and who knew something of the Abbey's history. Her friend confirmed that Newstead Abbey had once suffered a conflagration.

NORTH WILFORD POWER STATION

In December 1989 Tom Perrott and I attended a two day course and lectures on the paranormal at Pyke House, Battle, in East Sussex. Our Tutor was Tom's friend of long standing, the writer and parapsychologist, Andrew Green. Over drinks during a break in this enjoyable and informative weekend the subject of Nottinghamshire ghosts arose and one of the haunted locations referred to was the now demolished North Wilford Power Station. Andrew has included this in his book **Ghosts of Today.** I mentioned that a former colleague of mine was the grandson of one of the persons to witness the ghost there, a Mr. Sam Pykett, and I am grateful to Andrew for allowing me to record the story here.

The phantom which haunted, and perhaps continues to haunt the site of North Wilford Power Station, was encountered by Mr. Pykett in November 1967, when he was working a night shift. He had just shut down the pumps in the Screen Room when he thought that he heard something. At first he saw nothing but suddenly he saw a figure which smiled before turning and passing through a closed door. With this there came the realisation that he had become icy cold. Mr. Pykett subsequently described the apparition as being a 'little fellow wearing a check shirt, a blue bib overall and a cap. It had wide-set blue eyes and rather thick lips.'

Mr. Pykett entered his encounter in his daily report and also informed his foreman of it. This resulted in him being interviewed by senior members of the maintenance team who might have thought that he had imagined his experience. He convinced them that he had not. One of them, having again heard his description of the figure, supplied an interesting piece of information. The description given by Mr. Pykett fitted that of a former worker at the power station who had died some twenty five years previously and who was employed in the same capacity as Mr. Pykett. The phantom was later witnessed by another operative in the Turbine Room where it walked behind a pillar before disappearing. It continued to be seen from time to time until the power station was demolished several years ago.

YE OLDE BELL HOTEL BARNBY MOOR

In his novel **Rookwood,** written in 1834, Harrison Ainsworth tells how the notorious highwayman Dick Turpin rode to York. Folklore has it that he paused in his ride to rest his fictitious mare, Black Bess, at Ye Olde Bell Hotel at Barnby Moor, some two miles south-east of Blythe on the old Great North Road. Ainsworth makes no mention of this and Turpin, in fact, did not undertake that famous ride. It was performed by another highwayman, William Nevison, in about 1676.

Turpin's principal areas of operation were in the south but he ranged far and is believed to have committed a number of robberies on the Great North Road and as there are few inns of antiquity on former coaching routes that do not have associations with highwaymen, it is possible that he may have

visited the Bell at sometime during his career.

The Bell was described by one visitor in 1792 as 'the most comfortable and private public house, take it altogether that I was ever at.' This description still holds good today. During a recent visit I was told by a local businessman, a Mr. Barry Blenkiron, a patron for some 20 years and who once worked at the hotel in a maintenance capacity, of some of the eerie happenings that have occurred here.

The Nielson Room was originally a part of the old stables. Some years ago when this was undergoing renovation Mr. Blenkiron was working in there one evening when he felt a tug at his collar. He did not turn round as he assumed that one of the returning workmen was responsible. When this happened again some moments later he turned to confront the prankster. He found no-one. Most are familiar with the expression 'my hair stood on end.' Mr. Blenkiron, until his experience, considered this to be nothing more than a figure of speech. He hurriedly left the room but, being of a practical nature, returned some moments later in order to try to discover a logical explanation for his experience. This he was unable to do.

It is rumoured that in the long distant past a guest committed suicide by hanging himself in one of the bedrooms of the Bell. One night several years ago Mr. Blenkiron was working in the corridor near to this room when one of the chambermaids paused to chat with him. Some moments later she entered this room and he heard her addressing someone to the effect that, 'would he mind if she turned down the coverlet of the bed.' Within seconds she came hurrying towards him in a state of fright. He managed to calm her and she explained that after she had left him she had followed a man into the room, but when they went inside 'he was suddenly no longer there.' As a result of this experience she terminated her employment the following week.

Whilst working abroad Mr. Blenkiron's daughter, Julie, a receptionist at the Bell, happened to meet a gentleman who regularly stayed overnight when he had business in the area. During their conversation he told her that he had once booked into this room. He was unaware of its reputation. Within moments of entering he had found the atmosphere to be so disquieting that he refused to spend the night in it. I have, for obvious reasons, omitted to mention the number of this room.

My telephone conversation with the Bell's duty manager, Mr. John Houseman, revealed that he had experienced an inexplicable happening at the hotel one night in 1988. After the staff had left the premises he was preparing a conference table in the Bradgate Room. He left the room for a few moments to collect something, and on his return he discovered that all the glassware had been moved to the centre of the table.

The Bell appears to be haunted by a 'grey lady' which has been witnessed in the ballroom. A retired porter insists that even during the summer months areas in here were always extremely cold and several former members of the staff claim to have seen this grey, wraith-like figure at night, not only in the ballroom, but also on the stairs and in the corridors.

THE FLYING HORSE HOTEL NOTTINGHAM

In February 1987 the *Nottingham Evening Post* included a feature to mark the closure of one of the city's best known public houses, the Flying Horse Hotel situated in The Poultry. Following alterations and refurbishment the premises reopened as a shopping arcade.

The Flying Horse displayed the date 1483 but it is by no means certain that this is when the building opened as an inn although there was a Flying Horse in 1618 and probably earlier, possibly built or rebuilt around 1600 and an inn by 1740. The original building was a private residence, built in 1392 and which belonged to the Plumptre family.

Over the centuries many alterations were made to the Flying Horse and during the 18th century it was a busy coaching inn popular with travellers bound for London. It was also the headquarters of the Tory Party. The name 'Flying Horse' is thought to have been derived from a swinging horse, its rider swinging to and fro whilst attempting to take a ring from a quintain with a sword. This was a popular entertainment at medieval fairs. Considering the antiquity of these premises it would be surprising if they were not reputed to be haunted.

Some years ago a guest was staying in room number 29. During the night he came downstairs in some agitation and refused to return to his room. He had seen a 'lady in grey' in the corridor. Perhaps it was this phantom which is said to have touched a member of staff on the shoulder when he was in the beer cellar but which had disappeared when he turned round. On one occasion the telephone in the Friar Tuck restaurant, which was empty and secured from the rest of the premises, contacted the switchboard. When the assistant manager investigated he discovered all the lights to be burning but found no-one in the room. Such then, are some of the ghost stories told about the Flying Horse Hotel.

YE OLDE SALUTATION INN

On 3rd July 1988, I conducted the original guided tour to visit several of the county's historic and reputedly haunted buildings referred to in *'Haunted Nottinghamshire.'* *Nottingham Evening Post* feature writer and columnist Caroline Stringer very kindly accepted my invitation to join this and subsequently wrote an excellent feature to record the occasion. With the kind permission of licencees Barry and Beverley Bloom I was able to include on the itinerary a visit to Ye Olde Salutation Inn on Houndsgate, Nottingham.

Ye Olde Salutation Inn, or 'The Sal' as it is known to its habitués, dates from the 15th century and in the entrance passageway its worn flagstones bear testimony to the generations that have quaffed at this medieval inn. It has what is perhaps the finest example of a cave system in Nottingham which is thought to have been a part of a Saxon dwelling. In bygone days these have served a variety of purposes, from a tannery to brewing ale, and they include an ancient well.

By tradition the inn was, in the 18th century, much frequented by highwaymen. Here the 'gentlemen of the road' are said to have caroused, freely spending their illicit gains on doxies and wine after which empty purses caused them to look to their pistols, swing into the saddle, and set forth once more to conduct their nefarious 'profession' on the King's highway.

Mr. David Flint, who shows interested parties round the caves of the inn and is knowledgeable about its long history, told me that the ghost of a former landlord, who inadvertently poisoned himself some centuries ago, is said to haunt the premises but had not been seen for many years. David had not experienced anything of a ghostly nature at Ye Olde Salutation Inn, but, in 1984 a friend of his did.

His friend, who was unaware that the inn was reputed to be haunted, had volunteered to help him with the restoration of the caves. After some hours David went upstairs for refreshment. His friend said that he would shortly join him. Some minutes later he fled from the cellar. He was almost incoherent with fright and hurriedly left the inn.

When David telephoned him later that day to enquire as to what had happened to cause him to leave with such urgency, his friend, now composed, quietly explained that he had looked up from his work to see a figure. This was attired in a 'tricorn hat, lace jabot, and a riding coat with a brace of pistols in its belt'. This was, of course, the traditional apparel of the 18th century highwayman.

COLWICK HALL HOTEL

Throughout the British Isles white, grey, blue and green ladies continue to roam the houses they knew in life. The White Lady of Colwick Hall, as far as is known, has never been encountered inside the hotel. It confines its appearance to the grounds where it was seen in recent years by a diner, and it has also been witnessed near the ruin of Colwick Church. It does however, from time to time make its presence felt, particularly in the east wing. Mrs. Margaret Swift told me that when she worked as a waitress at the hotel she had sensed a presence when in the east wing and had felt the atmosphere suddenly become cold on numerous occasions, especially during the months of October and November. She also mentioned a supposed secret passage which led from this wing to the ruined church.

Mr. Ron Williams, a former manager, informed me that when he and his wife took up the post they were told by the locals of the White Lady, and of eerie happenings at the hotel, but as they were both 'disbelievers in ghosts' they had dismissed the stories. However, certain areas of the building were always found to be inordinately cold and the staff, after returning from the east wing, would complain of 'being watched.' This, he ascribed to their imagination.

Mr. Williams' first intimation of something strange at the hotel was his discovery of the cellar door which, after being secured, was found open. This was, he initially thought, due to a lapse of memory on his part. When this recurred on several occasions he began to wonder if there was some truth to the stories of the hotel being haunted. The domestic quarters were adjacent to the east wing and it was due to an inexplicable incident there that he realised there was some substance in the stories. Their living quarters when unoccupied, were kept locked, but one morning Mr. & Mrs. Williams entered and discovered that an ottoman chest had been turned round so that the front of the chest was facing the wall. They were, of course, mystified by this. Some time afterwards guests requested to see the upper floors of the hotel and, after unlocking the door, they found that the ottoman had again been moved. These incidents were the first of many which occurred periodically during their five year stay.

On one occasion Mr. & Mrs. Williams were awakened at dawn by the sound of a young woman sobbing, which seemed to emanate from the east wing. Mr. Williams, thinking that someone had been locked in there overnight hurried downstairs, but as he inserted the key and began to unlock the door the sobbing promptly ceased. A search of not only the east wing but also of the entire building revealed nothing.

Mr. Williams once came home to find his wife in a state of shock. She had, it transpired, let the kitchen porter out of the front door and then locked it behind him. After tidying the lounge bar she noticed a short time later that the front door was open. Ascending the stairs she suddenly realised that she was alone in the building. Therefore, who was responsible for opening the door? Mr. Williams found her, still on the staircase, afraid to go up or down, when he arrived some hours later. He searched the hotel and the grounds but found no-one.

A dwelling has stood on the site of Colwick Hall for centuries and the present house, built in 1776 and much renovated by the Home Brewery in 1973, has had many owners, thus the identity of its white lady must remain speculative. Locals believe it to be the phantom of Mary Ann Chaworth, Byron's 'Morning star of Annesley' who, in 1806 married John Musters the sporting squire of Colwick and Wiverton, when the name Chaworth was then hyphenated to Chaworth-Musters. This belief is attributed to events which took place in Nottingham during October of 1831, when the Reform Bill rioters marched on Colwick Hall. They caused superficial damage whilst the only occupants of the house, Mary Ann Chaworth-Musters and a lady companion, took refuge in the shrubbery, a course of action which was to prove fatal for Mary Ann. The exposure which she suffered brought about her death at Wiverton Hall some months later.

Did her ghost return to Colwick Hall or is the wraith occasionally glimpsed in the grounds and which makes its presence felt in the east wing that of a female whose identity and fate history has not recorded? Whatever its identity, most people feel that the White Lady of Colwick Hall is a sad and harmless phantom, to be pitied rather than feared.

MANVERS ARMS
RADCLIFFE-ON-TRENT

In the large village of Radcliffe-on-Trent, opposite St. Mary's Church, is a former coaching inn, the Manvers Arms. The inn stands on the site of the White Hart whose cellars were incorporated into the present structure which dates from 1792. Nearby are the old whipping posts.

Within living memory a shed once stood at the rear of the house which is said to have been used as a temporary mortuary for some of the many victims claimed by the nearby River Trent. It is believed locally that the cellars of the Manvers Arms were also utilised as a mortuary by the church, with beer barrels stored on one side and corpses on the other. In these cellars are two bricked up entrances behind which are thought to be tunnels leading to St. Mary's.

Not surprisingly, considering its macabre associations, the Manvers Arms is reputed to be haunted and a number of licencees have experienced disturbing and inexplicable happenings at the premises. Beer barrels have been found to be mysteriously moved and one former landlady entered her bedroom to discover her dresses folded neatly over chairs.

The present licencees, Chris and Karen Britton, have also experienced some strange occurrences such as the occasion when two half-pint glasses, which were stacked on a shelf behind the bar, suddenly moved and smashed on to the floor. This incident was witnessed and confirmed by two of the regulars, both local businessmen, with whom I have spoken. Chris has also wakened during the night and, although he has seen nothing, has 'sensed something' in the room.

Chris and Karen's boxer dog is reluctant to venture into the cellars where a relief landlady recently claimed to have felt something akin to a cold hand touch her face. In 1988 on Halloween night, Chris and a friend spent the night in the cellars in order to raise money for Shipstones' Christmas appeal for the City Hospital's childrens' ward. This proved to be uneventful but during the small hours they both smelt a 'strange musty odour — like old sacking.'

With permission from Chris and Karen, the Nottingham Psychical Research Group, accompanied by my friend Dennis Moyses of The Ghost Club, conducted an all night investigation in the cellars of the Manvers Arms on the 7th December 1988. Unfortunately, our equipment registered no abnormalities, and the night passed, as have the majority of our investigations, without incident.

SHERWOOD FOREST

Since time immemorial forests and woodlands have been believed to be the abode of preternatural beings. Even in this 'enlightened' age whilst certain kinds of tree continue to be venerated by those with an understanding of tree lore, others are shunned in the belief that they are inhabited by elementals or malignant entities.

Nottinghamshire's famous Sherwood Forest once covered approximately one fifth of the county. In his book **Haunted Britain,** the late Elliott O'Donnell records that as late as the nineties of the last century an area of this forest was said to be haunted by an invisible presence. This spot caused such terror that people dare not pass it even during the daytime. It gave them the impression of being strangled.

PHANTOM PASSENGERS

The urban legend of the phantom hitch-hiker is known to many. The hitch-hiker, usually female, is given a lift and gives the driver the address of her home. During the journey she suddenly disappears. When the motorist arrives at the address he is informed that his mysterious passenger had once lived there but had died in a motoring accident some years previously on the stretch of road where he had stopped to pick her up.

A variation on this theme is that of the vanishing bus passenger. An issue of the now discontinued *Nottingham Guardian Journal* records that a man once boarded a late bus outside Redhill Cemetery on Mansfield Road, Arnold. He went upstairs but when the conductress went to collect his fare she found no-one. When the bus reached Mansfield it was searched by the police but they too found the top deck unoccupied.

A HOUSE IN SHERWOOD

From 1979 until 1984 a banker, his wife and four children, experienced inexplicable happenings at a large Victorian house in Sherwood, Nottingham. This house has associations with a famous but controversial Nottinghamshire writer. It was the couple's youngest son who, shortly after the family had taken up residence, experienced the first of the many strange happenings which persisted throughout their occupation of the property.

One morning he went into the kitchen where he saw a figure attired in an 'old fashioned maids uniform' and which appeared to be mixing something in a bowl. He left the room and called for his mother. When she arrived he told her of what he had seen but when she went into the kitchen the figure was no longer there. When their eldest son was in the kitchen late one night there was a sudden flash and he experienced a 'strange sensation' and that of 'something rushing by.' Over the ensuing years another female figure in a Victorian dress was seen, usually in the vicinity of the staircase. On one occasion whilst sitting in the drawing room early in the evening the family heard footsteps running across the terrace. The banker and his eldest son investigated but found no-one.

These events were, I am told, irritating rather than frightening, especially the periodic disappearance of the children's toys and clothes which, despite a thorough search, were never found. The disturbances were always at their most active at the changing of the seasons, particularly in the Spring.

In an endeavour to find an explanation for these happenings a psychical research organisation (now disbanded) was invited to conduct an investigation at the house. During the investigation it was discovered that the children's playroom, which was situated at the top of the house and which the family's dog was always reluctant to enter, had a considerable difference in temperature from that of the corridor outside. In the garden a short time later, examining the area where the footsteps were heard, members of the family and of the psychical research organisation happened to glance up at the window of the playroom where they saw a figure looking down at them. Both a search of this room and the investigation proved to be inconclusive.

JESSE'S RESTAURANT

This popular restaurant in Goosegate, Hockley, is aptly named. The titles of the dishes on its menu with their pharmaceutical connotations reflect its associations with one of Nottinghamshires most famous men, Lord Trent, perhaps better known as Jesse Boot. These premises once housed his first shop. Many buildings, often erroneously, are said to be haunted by the phantom of a famous former owner or by that of someone who had associations with the property. Whilst there is nothing to suggest that the shade of Jesse Boot haunts this building, in 1988, shortly after the restaurant opened, its manager Mr. Neale Meyers (who is also a qualified chemist), together with a waiter, had an experience here for which an explanation could not be found and which might be construed as paranormal.

Neale related to me how one night while they were enjoying a drink after the last diners had left and the premises were secured, they felt a slight but distinct drop in temperature. Neale left the room to increase the heating and shortly after his return they both heard footsteps which began on the floorboards of the dining area and which crossed onto the tiled floor near the bar. They were then heard to pass along the corridor and into the office.

Although Neale and his companion saw no-one they assumed that an intruder was on the premises and a search was made, but without success. During his subsequent enquiries, in an attempt to find an explanation for this incident, he was told that 'it happened all the time.'

THE 'SUNKEN CHURCH' BRAMCOTE

It is always gratifying for a psychical researcher to receive reports of phenomena or reputedly haunted buildings, especially when these are from independent sources referring to the same location. Two Bramcote residents, a Mrs. Runa Tomlinson and a Mr. Lynmoor, both contacted me to say that the 13th century church tower opposite Cow Lane, which is known locally as the 'Sunken Church,' is reputed to harbour a phantom monk. My subsequent research revealed that although the church is without monastic associations, in 1978, P.C. Graham Wilkins, the then village policeman, did witness a strange figure here. With the help and co-operation of the Nottinghamshire Constabulary I was able to meet P.C. Wilkins. Here is an account of his experience at the 'sunken church.'

'I arrived at Cow Lane between 12.30am and 1.00am. When I was some 35 yards away from the church something

in the churchyard caught my eye. It was a figure without a definite outline but it appeared to be a human form. I could not define what it was and assumed it to be a shadow. I continued to observe it when it moved some ten yards to my right and then it stopped by a gravestone. I shone my torch at the figure. The torch beam shone through it and illuminated the gravestone behind it. It then started towards me. It did not walk but moved with a gliding motion. I then crossed over the road towards the figure and on my reaching the centre of the road it stopped and then retreated towards a gravestone. Whilst continuing to observe the figure I radioed my Inspector. Some minutes later I heard the sound of an approaching vehicle and I was relieved to see that it was a police car. When I looked again at the churchyard the figure was no longer there. I explained to my Inspector what had happened and we searched the churchyard. There was no sign of the figure but as there was dew on the grass we expected to find some footprints. There were none.'

P.C. Wilkins described this figure to me as being 'between 5 feet 8 or 10 inches tall. It wore a black ankle length coat and wore some sort of hat. It was not a cowl or hood but something like a three cornered hat with a high collar pulled up beneath it. I was unable to see its face.'

Shortly after his experience P.C. Wilkin's wife was visited by an elderly local gentleman. He informed her that her husband had witnessed a phantom coachman. P.C. Wilkins called on him and was told that many years ago a female servant who was employed at one of Bramcote's large houses was murdered by a coachman. His remorse was such that before he could be brought to justice he committed suicide somewhere in the vicinity of the 'Sunken Church.' His body is believed to have been buried in unconsecrated ground and it is his ghost which haunts this area and is sometimes mistaken for that of a monk.

P.C. Wilkins later learned that when two policemen were motoring late one night towards a bend a short distance beyond the 'Sunken Church' (known locally as 'the Devil's Elbow') they also witnessed this ghostly figure.

THE MANOR HOUSE, BRAMCOTE

The owners of The Manor House, Bramcote, Mr. and Mrs. D. W. J. Little, told me that their home is reputed to be haunted by the happy ghost of a teenage girl attired in a blue dress and which is also said to have been witnessed in their garden. Mr. and Mrs. Little have lived here for 15 years but they themselves have not yet seen this phantom.

GONALSTON MILL

In the quaint village of Gonalston, by the side of the stream called the Dover Beck and veiled by trees, stands a superbly renovated cotton mill, now a private residence, which has long been reputed to be haunted. This reputation stems from days when its workforce consisted largely of children who endured a fourteen hour day, six days a week. It is said that many, owing to the harsh treatment they received, died, and were buried, without ceremony, in the grounds.

I have spoken with people who aver that prior to the mill's restoration its grounds had an uninviting atmosphere and where, occasionally, children's cries were heard. I have also been informed of a late motorist who claimed to have witnessed there the phantoms of two small boys in 'ragged clothing.'

A HOUSE IN BULWELL

An ocean of ink has been expended on the carnage known as The Great War. Although the guns fell silent over seventy years ago it would seem that the echoes of that genocide and the shades of its victims remain with us today . . . . . .

Following an invitation by Radio Trent presenter Rob Wagstaff to join him on his morning programme for a discussion about Nottinghamshire hauntings, I subsequently received some interesting telephone calls, one of which was from a general practice nurse, Mrs. Sandy Gavin.

Sandy spent much of her childhood at her maternal grandparents' Victorian terraced house on Gall Street, Bulwell. Late one afternoon as she began to ascend the stairs she saw, on the small landing, a mutilated and bloodied figure in a torn khaki uniform and a peaked hat on which rested a pair of smashed goggles. Sandy described this to her grandmother who told her that she had also seen this figure on a number of occasions. She believed it to be the ghost of her brother. During the First World War he had been a despatch rider who had been critically injured in an explosion. These injuries resulted in his death at a field hospital on the Somme.

RADIO TRENT 29/31 CASTLE GATE, NOTTINGHAM

Radio Trent broadcasts from a Georgian house, 29/31 Castle Gate, Nottingham. I was given an interesting tour of the premises by Rob Wagstaff who informed me that these were once a women's hospital and that the sound studios are in a former mortuary which was long believed to be haunted. In recent years there have been few paranormal happenings here but in 1975, perhaps owing to the structural alterations of the building when Radio Trent began broadcasting, these were a not uncommon occurrence.

John Peters told me how he once went into the sound studio to find a table shaking and where, on several occasions, he sensed a female presence, and once witnessed the apparition of an elderly woman with grey hair and clothed in antiquated night attire. More than one person has been touched by an invisible 'something' and doors opening and slamming shut in the night have been heard by security staff.

Guy Morris, a former Radio Trent presenter who is now with Sound FM in Leicester, told me that one night when he was on the air he saw at the periphery of his vision a 'tall black shadow resembling a Cromwellian soldier which suddenly disappeared.' Although this was in view for only a few seconds he was convinced that there was an intruder on the premises but his subsequent search revealed no-one.

These premises are largely undisturbed by such happenings today but should you happen one late night to be walking the narrow street in which they stand and chance to hear the clip clop of horses hooves and the rumble of carriage wheels, it might be best if you turned and retraced your steps. These sounds have been known to precede the appearance of a figure garbed in 19th century evening clothes and a top hat and which has been seen to melt through the door of 29/31 Castle Gate.

PHANTOM COACHES

We learn from ghostlore that spectral stagecoaches are not uncommon on the roads of England. Latter day reports of these apparitions are rare, but in 1990, a Mr. Barry McParland of Sutton-in-Ashfield, wrote to the local newspaper *Chad* about his sighting in the Kirkby Dumbles in 1984. He also enquired if anyone else had seen this phenomenon as he understood that it had been witnessed in this area by others.

Mr. McParland described how he had been walking his dog on a summer's day when he heard the sound of two galloping horses and had looked up to see two grey horses and a grey stagecoach manned by two grey drivers travelling along a grassy bank. His sighting lasted for some 12 seconds.

In the following edition of *Chad* there appeared a letter from a lady who had responded to his enquiry. She had not only heard about the phantom stagecoach but had herself witnessed it as had several of the older residents of the Pinxton area! It is thought to travel the old coach road and thence proceed across the fields to Brookhill Hall.

This letter, which was sent to Mr. McParland before being published in the *Chad,* is now in my possesion. In his reply to my request that I might include his experience here, he very kindly sent it to me together with another which he had received from a lady in Kirkby-in-Ashfield. His informant described how, some 30 years previously, her sister's mother-in-law had lived in an old farmhouse near to where Mr. McParland saw his apparition.

One night she heard the sound of horses and the rumble of a coach which stopped beneath her bedroom window. Her fear was such that she dare not leave her bed to investigate but she clearly heard the 'horses snorting' until the coach moved off.

An item about a phantom carriage and horses said to haunt the hill between Giltbrook and Newthorpe appeared in a 1922 edition of the *Nottingham Guardian Journal.* The writer of this article (identified only by the initials F.M.E.W.), had been told about this apparition in childhood and had all but forgotten about it until having good reason to recall the information some years later.

Accompanied by two companions the writer had had to make an urgent journey from Bulwell to Langley Mill, but being unable to obtain the usual public conveyance had taken a trap. Descending Gilt Hill at about midnight they saw a carriage, illuminated on each side by lamps, come speeding down Newthorpe Hill. The driver of their trap, wondering who could be driving in such a dangerous manner, quickly pulled over to the right into a hedge. The carriage bore down on them and the passengers thought that a collision was inevitable when it suddenly disappeared from sight.

Thinking that it had plunged over the hedge and into the brook they left their trap to make a search but found nothing. It was then that the writer remembered the story of the phantom carriage and pair and recalled that its driver was supposed to have lived at a large house somewhere in the vicinity and who was known to have driven recklessly. He was said to have been a disreputable character and was reputed to have broken his neck by being thrown over a hedge and into the brook which gives its name to Giltbrook.

PRIORY CHURCH OF ST. ANTHONY, OLD LENTON

This small church, partly Medieval, partly Victorian, stands on the site of the chapel of St. Anthony which served the hospital of Lenton Priory. Founded in the 12th century by William Peveril one of the most powerful men in the county, this great Cluniac monastery suffered the fate of many religious houses during the reign of Henry VIII when the last prior, together with several of the monks, was hanged.

It is a rewarding experience for both the layman and the historian to visit the Priory Church of St. Anthony for it contains a wealth of fascinating relics of the past. There is the 'leper's window,' a stone aperture through which those suffering from the disease could receive communion, and a stone fountain in which the priest would afterwards wash his hands. It has an oak panel bearing the Royal Arms of Charles I. After the king was executed Oliver Cromwell ordered all such heraldic signs to be destroyed. Lenton concealed the 'C' with an 'A' during the reign of Queen Anne and subsequently with a 'G' when George I ascended the throne. This resourcefulness came to light when the panel was being restored during the 1970's.

In 1945 Mrs. Ada Marriott was appointed verger of this church. Today, at the age of 80, it is a post which she still retains. Mrs. Marriott has twice seen a ghost here and several years ago a former vicar, at the request of the then deaconess performed the rite of exorcism in the church and its grounds. This, as is common with many exorcisms, seems to have been largely unsuccessful in that it appears to have had no lasting effect.

On numerous occasions Mrs. Marriott has sensed that there was someone in the church other than herself but saw no-one; prior to the exorcism she did see someone standing in the pulpit. Her immediate reaction was that it must have been a visitor to the church. She then became aware of the figure's antiquated apparel, 'a sort of cloak' and 'its small goatee beard and piercing eyes.' It then suddenly disappeared. Following the exorcism she saw the figure once more. It has since been witnessed by others including her daughter, Mrs. Glenys Randle, and people still claim to occasionally feel a 'presence' here.

Until recently an elderly friend of Mrs. Marriott lived at a house in Church Street, Old Lenton. Following a fall she was confined to bed. One morning she telephoned Mrs. Marriott and asked to see her. On arrival her friend told how she had awoken during the night to find a figure standing by her bedside. It informed her that she was not to worry, for her health would return. It then disappeared. Mrs. Marriot questioned her friend about the apparition and the description she was given matched that of the figure which she had seen inside the church. The phantom's prophecy proved to be correct for the lady did eventually make a full recovery from her injuries.

In 1977, the Lenton Local History Society of which Mrs. Glenys Randle is a member, was able to conduct an archaeological excavation on the site of Lenton Priory during which several skulls were unearthed. Glenys happened to notice that the ground near to where she was working suddenly began to crumble. Some ancient stonework and finger bones were revealed. She called to a colleague and they reported this to their supervisor from whom they received permission to excavate further. With much care more stonework and a complete skeleton were uncovered. The work was then suspended for several days until the skeleton could be examined by medical experts after which it was re-interred in the location where it was found. Glenys informed me that the skeleton was believed to be that of Sir William Babington, Chief Justice and Baron of the Exchequer. He died at the age of 99 and was buried at Lenton Priory in 1455.

GEDLING YOUTH CENTRE

This youth club is said to haunted by the ghost of a lady in a crinoline dress whose violet scented perfume sometimes permeates the premises. The centre is in a part of the old railway station and its ghost is believed to be that of a station master's wife who, at the turn of the century, following the death of her husband, committed suicide by throwing herself under a train.

Intrigued by this story, Youth Leader Mrs. Chris Cripwell attempted to verify it by checking the London and North Eastern Railway records pertaining to the station. Unfortunately these proved to be no longer extant and the visit of a colleague, to examine the records at the National Railway Museum, York, also proved fruitless.

That the premises do appear to be haunted, however, there seems little doubt, and as the phenomenon here occurs only during the month of September, this would indicate that it is of a cyclic nature. On several occasions lights have been reported burning late at night which has resulted in the police requesting Chris to unlock the premises in order that they might conduct a search, which of course, reveals no one.

Although none of the present Youth Leaders have witnessed the phantom, it was encountered on the stairs in recent years by a member. He described it as being that of a woman attired in a 'long white dress and with long straggly hair. It had no face.' 'He was ,' Chris told me, 'shaking like a leaf and it was two hours before he could be persuaded to return. There is no way that he could have been acting.'

On Saturday 23rd September 1989, the Nottingham Psychical Research Group was able to conduct an investigation at the centre in an attempt to record these inexplicable happenings. The area of the building where the member encountered the phantom was, in years gone by, the domestic quarters of the station. Chris told me that during a recent Youth Leaders' meeting the fluorescent light, which is operated by a cord, was suddenly extinguished and was then switched on again. This, understandably, caused some consternation.

We commenced our investigation in this room at 10.15pm but by 12.30am we had experienced nothing unusual, the cassette recorders we had placed in the other rooms revealed nothing of interest when played back. At 12.45am we returned downstairs to the area which had once been a part of the station's waiting room. Our examination of this revealed two 'cold spots.' These are thought to be indicative of phenomena, so we decided to spend some time here. It gradually, and not unnaturally, grew colder as the night progressed with nothing occurring until 1.17am when we heard a strange creaking noise. Old buildings are, of course, subject to many strange noises, for the most part structural, but this we agreed was reminiscent of the sounds produced by an antiquated railway signal. This was heard again at 2.28am. Its source could not be found. At 4.30am, as nothing further was heard and the 'cold spots' were no longer present we decided to leave.

Later that day I telephoned Chris to inform her of the results of our vigil and I enquired if she knew of any railway signals in the vicinity. She replied that the nearest, a modern one, was at least a mile and a half away, Sounds are, however, considerably amplified at night, especially during the small hours, thus, whatever was responsible for these noises, and the cold spots, must remain conjectural.

GEDLING HOUSE

Built in 1780, this elegant white house with its backdrop of hilly woodland is a familiar landmark to those who travel on the A612. It was once the home of Sir John Turney, a former Lord Mayor of Nottingham and the maternal grandfather of the writer Nicholas Monsarrat. In the 1960's it was purchased by the Nottinghamshire County Council to house the County

Education Resources Service. During the last war the house was occupied by the War Department Claims Commission and a lady who was stationed there during this period, told me of some of the strange occurrences which began shortly after the department took up residence.

She was amongst those, who, during the small hours, heard 'slow hesitant footsteps accompanied by a tapping sound in the upper regions of the house.' Then an unpleasant odour would permeate the building. The drains were, of course, examined but were found to be free of obstruction. It was thought that perhaps an animal had somehow found its way under the house where it had died and this resulted in the floorboards in several of the rooms being taken up so that a search could be made for a carcass. Strangely, although the search revealed nothing, the odour ceased.

During my visit to Gedling House I was told by the staff that although none of them had experienced anything untoward they had heard it was reputed to be haunted and suggested that I contact some former members of staff who might be able to help with my enquiry.

Former secretary Mrs. Elizabeth Williams told me that she was one of those fortunate people allowed to be accompanied by her dog whilst working. Mrs. Williams related how on one occasion she had left her office and was surprised to find her pet in the corridor. She then realised that her dog was still in the office and that she was being confronted by an apparition of a small white terrier which, within the space of a few seconds, faded away.

Mr. Derek Bilton is a retired museum services organiser who supervised the running of Gedling House for a number of years. He informed me that when he entered the house late one winter afternoon in 1967 his dog, which was usually well behaved, began to act in a strange manner then ran upstairs. He followed the animal into a certain room where, even when taking into account it was a winter's day, the room was still excessively cold. Some moments later the temperature fell even further when the room became imbued with a sweet fragrance. For some moments he was unable to move. He did not, however, feel endangered or threatened.

On more than one occasion Mr. Bilton heard the sound of ungainly footsteps together with a tapping noise and theorized that these sounds could indicate that the phantom of Gedling House might be that of a disabled person. In 1968, he witnessed in a room on the second floor, the ghost of an elderly woman with a walking stick accompanied by a small white dog. The figures remained in view for only a few moments before fading away.

A short distance beyond Gedling House, enclosed by a high wall which ensures privacy, is a large but strangely silent and brooding overgrown garden. I was told by one local resident that it is rumoured that many years ago black magic was practised here. It is a place where few now care to linger.

HOLME PIERREPONT HALL

As one travels the A52, Holme Pierrepont Hall, together with its church of St. Edmund, can be glimpsed standing in isolated seclusion a short distance from Radcliffe-on-Trent. This splendid house has long been the home of the Pierrepont

41

family and is still owned by their descendants.

Some 20 years ago a Mr. Paul Hope of Radcliffe-on-Trent regularly visited its park in order to pursue his interest in ornithology. On one occasion, in the late afternoon nearing dusk, he saw what appeared to be a woman attired in a long greyish-white dress. The figure walked from a gate up to the house and back again several times before it inexplicably disappeared. Mr. Hope estimated that the figure was in view for approximately 10 minutes. It was not until some five years later that he learned that the park was said to be haunted by a 'White Lady.' Mr. Hope, however, does not claim that what he saw was a phantom as he cannot be certain what it was.

Another gentleman from Radcliffe-on-Trent, a local shopkeeper, informed me that he had also witnessed a similar figure on several occasions when driving past the Hall at night. His father had seen this figure many years previously as, it is alleged, had some soldiers when billeted at the Hall during the last war. However, my correspondence with its owner, Mr. Robin Brackenbury, revealed that he has neither witnessed nor experienced anything of a supposed paranormal nature at Holme Pierrepont Hall.

THRUMPTON HALL

Some eight miles south-west of Nottingham, serene and dignified Thrumpton Hall is situated amongst trees in a secluded spot close by the River Trent. Thrumpton Hall dates largely from 1607 but it incorporates parts of a much older house which belonged to the staunch Roman Catholic family, the Powdrills. The house contains a priest's hole at the foot of a secret staircase and this was used by the family to conceal Father Garnett, one of the principal participants in the Gunpowder Plot of 1605. This resulted in Thrumpton Hall being confiscated. Their successors, however, the Pigot family, lost the house some 90 years later.

It was the second Gervase Pigot who, during the reign of Charles II, added one of the most notable features of the house, the magnificent and richly carved staircase, known as The Grand Staircase. As a result of his ambitious plans for the house and consequent overspending, Pigot had to remortgage the estate and in 1694 John Emerton foreclosed it and took possession since when Thrumpton Hall has descended from him but never directly from father to son.

Thrumpton Hall is owned by The Hon. Mr. and Mrs. George FitzRoy Seymour. Mr. Seymour, nephew of the 10th Lord Byron, told me that neither he nor his wife had ever witnessed phantoms in their home but they had 'sensed things,' usually simultaneously and when on The White Staircase. Mr. Seymour described this as being 'of someone behind one' and, when sitting in the library, of hearing footsteps in the Saloon, situated above the library.

A former head housemaid however, a Miss Lynn, did encounter a mysterious figure on The Grand Staircase. This was dressed in the manner of a cavalier and others have also witnessed this same figure in the Saloon which is in the vicinity of Miss Lynn's sighting.

From 1838 until her death in 1912 at the age of 88, Thrumpton Hall was owned by Lucy, Lady Byron. She was married to the Hon. George Byron, later the 8th Lord Byron, the son of the poet's first cousin. This lady was an accomplished musician of some repute and much of her beautifully bound sheet music remains in the house. Mr. Seymour once overheard his daughter, who frequently plays the piano in the library, telling an elderly friend that sometimes when playing this particular music that she has felt a hand touch her on the shoulder and 'then I play much better.'

CONTROL TOWER, WIGSLEY

During the Second World War there were over 700 airfields in England. Today, many lie abandoned with weed-choked runways, their buildings lying in ruins or demolished. Often all that remains is the stark, decaying shell of the control tower, such as the one at Wigsley. Were it not for this, one would be

unaware that an airfield had existed here.

Some years ago, during a party at 'The Lodge,' a nearby house on Wigsley Road, I was informed that the control tower was reputed to be haunted and from where it is said that sometimes, on still nights, the faint sounds of morse code may be heard. The Nottingham Psychical Research Group have subsequently visited it on several occasions but without hearing this. Nevertheless, this brooding three storied building has an extraordinary atmosphere and the shards of broken glass which have fallen from its rusted window frames crunching underfoot and one's footsteps echoing on its stone staircases seem to heighten one's awareness of this. Perhaps it is this atmosphere which has caused more than one curious visitor to leave hurriedly.

THE BLIDWORTH BOULDER

A footpath meanders over several fields before reaching the proximity of this stark isolated stone which stands some 15 feet high. It is known as the Blidworth Boulder and it is said to have had associations with Druids and their mysterious rituals. There is no documented evidence to support this belief as the Celts had no written history. Druids, for the most part, practiced their rites in forest clearings, particularly near oak trees which they worshipped; but the experience here of one Blidworth resident might indicate some validity in the belief that in the mists of antiquity the stone may well have been the site of pagan practices.

In the May of 1990 my informant was taking an evening stroll accompanied by his dog. Habit dictated that on reaching the stone he would stop for a rest and enjoy a cigarette before returning home. His dog usually took this opportunity to search for rabbits but on this occasion it seemed reluctant to leave his side. Some moments later its hackles rose, and staring at the stone, it began to growl. He saw nothing to account for its behaviour but with a surge of fear he suddenly became aware of the unnatural silence in the area and of the conviction that he and his pet were not alone.

Quickly attaching the dog's lead to its collar he began to hurry homeward, his dog now and then pausing to turn and growl as if something were following. Each time he glanced backwards he saw nothing, but the feeling of being stalked remained. It was not until they reached the first stile of the footpath that the dog began to behave normally and where he felt they were no longer being followed. He still occasionally walks his dog to the Blidworth Boulder — but takes care to leave before nightfall.

WOLLATON HALL

Designed by architect Robert Smythson and built by Sir Francis Willoughby between 1580 and 1588, this impressive Elizabethan mansion houses one of the finest natural history museums in the country and it attracts some 250,000 visitors each year. Wollaton Hall is, of course, reputed to have its ubiquitous 'White Lady' which is said to walk the 'half roof.' Her spectral form has ceased to cause concern for it has not been seen for many years; but one does not need to witness a phantom to be made aware of the paranormal; echoes of things long forgotten, heard or sensed can also inspire fear.

In his reply to my enquiry about supposed inexplicable happenings at Wollaton Hall, Mr. Graham Walley, Senior Keeper (Natural Sciences), informed me that although the house has a pleasant unthreatening atmosphere a few of its visitors have occasionally felt uncomfortable in certain rooms and that some responsible members of the staff have twice heard a 'heavy breathing sound' and footsteps which, seemingly, were without cause. Mr. Don Sharp who has been the museum's chief taxidermist for 26 years and whose work is displayed here, kindly invited my wife and me to discuss some of these incidents with him.

Mr. Sharp told us that in 1970 the house had had a new heating system installed. Three contractors were working in the north-east tower where, unbeknown to them, some visitors claimed to have heard the sound of children crying. Late one afternoon one of the men came downstairs and, in a state of considerable agitation, promptly terminated his employment. He explained that he had been working alone in a room of this tower and had been shocked to hear the tread of disembodied footsteps. He could not be persuaded to rescind his decision,

The south-east tower has a room that was once used for displaying fossils and where, for no apparent reason, a number of people have fainted. Following its refurbishment, this has ceased to happen. Several people have witnessed what is variously described as a mist or smoke in the minstrels' gallery and which always drifts from left to right before disappearing. This has occurred quite recently and was witnessed by two museum attendants. They each ascended a staircase to investigate but, on reaching the gallery, they found that the mist was no longer there.

Mr. Sharp's roomy workshop with its fascinating array of future exhibits currently under construction is in a former kitchen. He has worked alone and far into the night on numerous occasions and, owing to his environment, is well aware of the strange sounds that may be heard in large old houses. He explained that when one is engrossed in one's work these go largely unnoticed. However, one night some fifteen years ago he heard the sound of footsteps slowly descending the stone staircase which is adjacent to his workshop. These proceeded across the stone flagged hall and halted outside his workshop door. He knew that the house had been secured and realised that there must be an intruder on the premises. A sensation of sudden coldness then swept over him and, picking up a hammer, he threw open the door to confront the prowler. He found no-one and a search of the staircase and corridor, during which the atmosphere remained inordinately cold, also failed to reveal anyone. He quickly left the house and it was some months before he would work again after dark.

Although Mr. Sharp does not believe in ghosts in the accepted sense of the word he does feel that 'there is, in some form, a presence at Wollaton Hall.'

MATTERSEY PRIORY

Tranquil, isolated, and one of the least visited English Heritage properties, the remains of this ancient Priory are situated by the side of the gently flowing River Idle and are reached by means of a lengthy unadopted road. Founded in 1185, Mattersey Priory was a small monastic house of the

Gilbertine order, the only house of that order in the county, which housed a group of six regular canons. Its exposed ground plan reveals the remains of the cloister, parts of the refectory and chapel together with the vestiges of two altars.

When businessman Mr. Brian Perry purchased the former farmhouse which overlooks these fragments of the past he was informed locally that they are believed to be haunted. Some five years later Mr. Perry and his family have yet to see a ghost here and my enquiries failed to trace anyone in the village who would vouch to having witnessed a phantom in the ruins. Word of my enquiries did, however, reach the attention of a lady who lives in Retford and who consequently telephoned me about her experience there.

She had visited Mattersey Priory on numerous occasions, sometimes to enjoy its serene atmosphere and on others to sketch. It was on a latter occasion in February 1989 that she had her only encounter with 'something out of the ordinary.' Arriving shortly after 3.00pm she began sketching but on several occasions during the afternoon she felt that she was being watched. Each time she looked up from her work she saw no-one. When the light began to fade such that she could no longer sketch accurately she prepared to leave. It was then when walking towards her car, that she heard a faint but distinct chanting emanating from the ruins. She·paused to listen and on turning saw a 'dark cowled figure, of middle height,' which appeared to be observing her standing by one of the few remaining walls. She was not, the lady assured me, in the least afraid as she approached the figure, which seemed to fade into the wall when the chanting ceased. Although she saw only a single figure, the chanting seemed to comprise several voices.

When I telephoned Dennis Moyses about my initial visit to Mattersey Priory, and about its reputation, he was eager to accompany the Nottingham Psychical Research Group on its proposed vigil there. This was arranged for Saturday 28th April 1990. Arriving at 11.30pm we found the ruins to be bathed by the light of a sickle moon and the night was still save for the occasional cry of nocturnal creatures and the faint hum of distant traffic. We distributed thermometers and cassette recorders amongst the ruins, paying particular attention to the area where the lady had seen her phantom. By 4.00am the late traffic had ceased, the moon was obscured by cloud, and our surroundings were cloaked in darkness. The night became bitterly cold. We saw no cowled figures and the night remained undisturbed by chanting. We felt compensated for this by the unique atmosphere of Mattersey Priory which will remain on our files as one of the properties which the group will periodically visit in the hope that one night our patience will be rewarded when we also might experience a playback of the past.

WORKSOP PRIORY

There are many buildings which, because of their antiquity, are said to be haunted. Such is the reputation of Worksop Priory, founded by William de Lovetot c1120. In its edition of 15th January 1988, the *Worksop Guardian* included an article about its supposed ghosts and this included the opinions of local people together with some of their experiences of albeit strange, but not necessarily paranormal, happenings there.

"I don't think there is a ghost at the Priory, although I have

49

heard rumours," said the secretary at the Priory and, according to the verger, 'It's a load of nonsense, but there's supposed to be a monk who walks the transept in the church on Midsummer's Eve and people have reported the sound of footsteps when no-one is actually there.' Tunnels lead from the Priory to the Lion Hotel, a Georgian house on Bridge Street, and there have also been reports of phantom monks walking in these.

An interview with the flower arranger at the Priory revealed that she had once constructed a large floral display in one of the transepts. She had considered it to be stable. The church had been secured for the night but the following morning the display was found to have fallen to the floor and was ruined.

The Lady Chapel which survived the dissolution when the monastic parts of the church were pulled down, is where a woman clothed in blue has been seen who suddenly vanishes. A regular visitor to the Priory related how he had once been walking towards the Lady Chapel, 'the most sacred part of the church, when the door unlatched itself and slowly re-closed. There are usually no draughts in the Lady Chapel and I was so astonished and bewildered that I turned and slowly walked away'.

The *Worksop Guardian* concluded this article by asking

its readers to form their own opinions about the Priory being haunted and by saying that it would be interested in any stories about a ghost there. This prompted a number of replies which were published in its January 29th edition and included one from a young man who had claimed to have seen a blue lady on 12 occasions.

His first encounter was in the June of the previous year. Walking past the Priory late at night he saw 'a shining light so I went to look around. At the back of the church, at the top end of the graveyard, I saw a blue figure. She was an oldish lady, about 75 and had an unhappy expression on her face. She also had something on her head.' He quickly left but has continued to see this figure walking in the Priory grounds. He told his friend about his experience and he replied that he had also felt a 'ghostly presence' and had seen 'something' sitting in a tree.

This article also included a report from a lady who had been a pupil of the Abbey Girls' School and with whom I have subsequently spoken. She had been one of the pupils who had had some of their lessons in the Priory Gatehouse which dates from the 14th century. Its ghosts are said to include a crusader, a monk, a nun, a white lady and a blue lady. Although she had seen none of these phantoms she recalled that she and her school friends would talk about a blue lady who would sit on a 'funny shaped tree just down from the Gatehouse.'

PUMP HOUSE, MISTERTON SOSS

Green ladies, together with their spectral sisters of the white, grey, brown and blue varieties are, for the most part, largely associated with historic country houses, thus a disused Victorian pump house would seem to be an unlikely place in which to encounter one of these phantoms. Yet, there are those who live in the village of Misterton who allude to a

Green Lady which is believed to haunt this isolated and derelict building by the side of the River Idle.

It is said that one night many years ago a lady was making her way to her cottage on the river bank. Owing to fog which often shrouds this area she became disorientated and stumbled into the river. When the pump house was activated the following morning her body, which had been swept into it by the current, was brought to the surface of the water.

The most recent sighting of what may have been this phantom occurred on an April night in 1990. I was informed that a courting couple had parked their car by the side of the pump house and that after a while the young man's curiosity about the building had prompted him to visit it. His girlfriend had chosen to remain in the car. Some ten minutes later he rushed back to the vehicle and, with fumbling fingers, started the engine and quickly drove off. He was obviously shaken but during the journey to his girlfriend's house he had refused to answer her questions about what had happened inside the old building. At her home he reluctantly explained that as he had stood inside the pump house he became aware that he was 'not alone.' He initially thought that his girlfriend had decided to join him for, in the gloom, he had seen the figure of a woman. He twice warned her to be careful as the building was dangerous underfoot and it would be easy to fall into the water. When she did not respond to his warnings his realisation grew of the figure's 'unnatural stillness' and of the 'sudden extreme coldness of the building.'

His girlfriend, being local, knew of the reputation of the pump house. As he lived in Gainsborough he had been unaware of this.

Into Derbyshire
WINGFIELD MANOR

Although this book is predominately about paranormal happenings in Nottinghamshire, I trust the reader will not object to taking a step into Derbyshire. Derbyshire has an abundance of historic houses a good many of which are, of course, reputed to be haunted. One of its most impressive, albeit largely ruined, is Wingfield Manor. Few can fail to be

stirred by the sight of this ancient and brooding house which dominates the countryside from its hilly location.

It was here in 1982 that the Nottingham Psychical Research Group, after hearing that the house was reputed to be haunted by phantom Parliamentarian soldiers, conducted one of its first all night vigils. Over the ensuing years the group has periodically conducted its investigations at Wingfield Manor, without to date witnessing phenomena. However, in his book *Ghosts in and Around Chesterfield* published in 1984, my friend the late Ray Pearson records that when some workmen were renovating the crypt (as Ray explains this is a misleading term; it was probably a food or wine store) one of them returned alone to his room and encountered a number of figures. These were attired in the manner of Cromwell's Ironsides.

During a visit, Tom Perrott and I were informed that when a medium/ghost buster visited Wingfield Manor, this person claimed that 'the walls spoke to me.' For us they remained mute! Incidentally how does one bust a ghost?

HIGHLOW HALL

My wife and I recently spent a long weekend at Highlow Hall, an ancient and isolated house near Hathersage. It stands behind a Tudor gateway by the side of a narrow and steeply winding lane. As I opened its iron-studded oak door, I reflected that we were entering what is considered by many inhabitants of the Hope Valley, to be perhaps the most haunted house in Derbyshire.

To the right of the entrance hall, where a grandfather clock chimed its welcome, are snug sitting rooms. On the left is the banqueting hall. This has an oak beamed ceiling, a flagstone floor, a Jacobean staircase and is dominated by a huge open fireplace. Highlow Hall is owned by a Mr. and Mrs. T. Wain and we were greeted by Mrs. Wain and shown to our room. This also had a large stone fireplace and from its leaded windows were magnificent views of dark brooding pine forests and a bleak moorland. Nearby are several tumuli and a stone circle known as Wet Withers. Later that evening Mrs. Wain told us something about the history of the house and of the phantoms which — by tradition — are reputed to haunt it.

The house was originally owned by the Archer family. When the last male Archer died in 1340 he left two daughters and both, unbeknown to the other, were being courted by Nicholas Eyre, a scion of the influential Eyre family of Hope. On his announcing his decision to marry the younger girl, the elder fled from the house and is believed to have committed suicide, thus originating Highlow Hall's best known ghost story. It is said that several years later her shade confronted Nicholas in the banqueting hall, accusing him of being responsible for her death and prophesying that for fifteen generations of Eyres all would be well, after which their fortunes would fail. That prophesy was fulfilled for after enjoying great wealth their fortunes did, eventually, suffer a decline which, in 1842, culminated in their estate being sold to the Duke of Devonshire. Perhaps it is this phantom said to be seen from time to time in the courtyard, attired in a long white dress with its hands resting on the cattle trough as if studying its reflection.

During the 16th century Highlow Hall was the home of Robert Eyre. He built or enlarged a similar house for each of his seven sons. All were situated in a strategic position thus enabling him, in the event of trouble in those turbulent times, to signal for their assistance. At sometime during the period of this construction work Robert discovered some of his masons playing dice. In the ensuing argument he drew his sword and killed one of the men whose phantom has since been said to walk Highlow Hall. It is believed that Nicholas Eyre also killed a workman when he became unable to tolerate the man's persistent complaining, and that the ghost of his victim also haunts the premises. This may, of course, be another variation of the story recorded above. Another supposed ghost at the house may be that of a friend of Nicholas Eyre. Following a drinking bout in Chesterfield the two men quarrelled en route to Highlow Hall and on arrival the hot tempered Nicholas killed his companion. He escaped the ultimate sentence of judicial retribution by claiming that he had acted in self defence.

Given Highlow Hall's reputation of being the abode of these numerous phantoms I enquired if Mrs. Wain had ever experienced anything of a ghostly nature in her home. She replied that she and her husband had lived in the house for over forty years and that neither they nor their children had witnessed a ghost there; neither had their succession of pets ever reacted in a manner which might suggest that phenomena were present. However, a lady who had spent a night at the house told Mrs. Wain the following morning that she would not be visiting Highlow Hall again. She explained that during the night she had seen two men in antiquated clothing fighting a duel and which had seemed to be occurring 'in the wall' of her room. Another female claimed to have seen a 'brown face' peering at her through a ground floor window!

Several years ago a television programme was made about ghosts and Highlow Hall was featured in this. The production team (who failed to record any paranormal activity) were accompanied to the house by a medium who told Mrs. Wain 'there is a presence here but it is benign.' Mediums are, of course, renowned for 'playing to the gallery.' After speaking with Mrs. Wain it would seem that Highlow Hall's reputation is based on the ghosts that were, and although Mr. and Mrs. Wain cannot guarantee that their guests will witness a phantom they can provide, in one of Derbyshire's oldest houses, a restful retreat for those who would seek to escape the tumult of the city.

Into Lincolnshire
HEMSWELL CLIFF HOTEL

This superbly renovated and comfortable hotel, the former officers' mess at Hemswell from where the Royal Air Force departed in 1967 is, today, almost unrecognisable as the ruinous building in which the Nottingham Psychical Research Group had conducted several of its investigations. Jack Lumsden and I first visited Hemswell in 1982 and were told by its caretaker, Mr. Stan Goodwin, that not only was the airfield reputed to be haunted but also the officer's mess which guard dogs would not enter.

Mr. Goodwin showed us round the building. It was in a dilapidated condition. Its most comfortable chamber was the billiard room and during our ensuing investigations here we would build a fire in its large hearth and used it as our 'base room,' leaving at intervals to conduct searches and to examine the recording instruments we had located throughout the building. Our investigations revealed no paranormal activity. Perhaps the phenomena reported to be here may be that of a transient or possibly cyclic nature.

Mr. Arthur Stowe previously ran a hotel in Lincoln and in 1985 he and his son, Chris, purchased the building. Together they undertook much of its restoration, often working during the night. They had been told that it was reputed to be haunted but had not experienced anything to substantiate this reputation. But on one occasion in the small hours, Chris was working in what is now the dining room when he had an impression of someone walking past the doorway and along the adjacent corridor. Though he saw nothing his conviction of this was such that he and his father made a search but to no avail. During an investigation in 1983 a guest of the Nottingham Psychical Research Group was in the corridor when he also experienced this.

ACKNOWLEDGEMENTS

Had it not been for the information given to me by many people this book could not have been written. I am particularly indebted to the following for their co-operation.

Mr. H. Aixhill, Mr. A. Ashworth, MBE., Mr. K. A. Barrett, Mr. D. Bilton, Mrs. W. Blanchard, Mr. B. Blenkiron, Mr. & Mrs. B. Bloom, Mr. J. Blott, Mr. R. Brackenbury, Mr. & Mrs. C. Britton, Mr. A. Congdon, Mrs. C. Cripwell, Mr. S. B. Critchlow, Mr. J. S. Daykin, Mr. D. Flint, Mrs. S. Gavin, Mr. S. Goodwin, P.c. D. Green, Mrs. O. Hayes, Mr. P. Hope, Mr. J. Houseman, Mr. & Mrs. D. W. J. Little, Mr. Lynmoor, Mrs. A. Marriott, Mr. B. McParland, Mr. N. Meyers, Mr. & Mrs. I. Moore, Mr. P. J. Naylor, Mrs. A. Pearce-Naylor, Mr. B. Perry, Mrs. G. Randle, Mrs. S. Rose, Mr. D. Rye, Mr. J. Rye, The Hon. Mr. & Mrs. G. FitzRoy Seymour, Mr. D. Sharp, Mr. R. Spencer, Mr. A. Stowe, Mr. C. Stowe, Mrs. M. Swift, Mrs. R. Tomlinson, Mr. & Mrs. T. Wain, Mr. O. J. Walker, Mr. G. Walley, Mr. S. White, P.c. G. Wilkins, Mrs. E. Williams, Mr. R. Williams, Mr. A. Wood.

My thanks also to Joan Forman, Mr. Barrie Williams, Editor of the Nottingham Evening Post and to Caroline Stringer, Mrs. Joy Turner and Mr. Angus Henderson of the Worksop Guardian, the editorial staff of the CHAD, the Managing Director of Radio Trent, Mr. C. Hughes, presenters Rob Wagstaff and John Peters, Mark Cummings of BBC Radio Nottingham, Guy Morris of Sound FM in Leicester, the staff of the local Studies Section County Library, Angel Row, Nottingham, Miss M. Clarke of the Nottingham University Library, English Heritage and the Nottinghamshire Constabulary.

I also wish to express my thanks and appreciation to my good friend and fellow bibliophile Tom Perrott, not only for his splendid and succinct foreword to this, but also for the many books he has given me, Andrew Green for his practical advice, my wife Jeanette for typing the manuscript and her support, Kevin Mee for providing the photographs and finally to all members of the Nottingham Psychical Research Group past and present, but especially to Major H. S. J. (Jack) Lumsden, Roy Westerman, Adrian Pearce-Naylor, Anthony Price and Dennis Moyses.

Each year I receive numerous applications for membership of the Nottingham Psychical Research Group. For a number of reasons its members prefer the group to remain small thus membership is limited to the most suitable applicants. For those who wish to learn about practical psychical research and who might wish to form their own group, I would recommend the study of these books.

'Ghost Hunting A Practical Guide', by Andrew Green
Published by The Garnstone Press Ltd., 1973

'The Ghost Hunter's Guide', by Peter Underwood
Published by Blandford Press, 1986

Both are also available in paperback.

INDEX

Ghosts & Legends Series -

DERBYSHIRE & THE PEAK DISTRICT -

DERBYSHIRE GHOSTS by Wayne Anthony Boylan . ISBN 0 946404 67 4

GHOSTS OF THE PEAK DISTRICT by Wayne Anthony Boyland.

STRANGE TALES OF THE PEAK by Richard Lichfield. ISBN.0 946404

THE ADVENTURES OF A BAKEWELL GOBLIN by Ben Andrews.

PEAK DISTRICT MONSTERS by Alan Smith.

LEGENDS OF DERBYSHIRE by John N. Merrill

DERBYSHIRE FOLKLORE by John N. Merrill

CUSTOMS OF DERBYSHIRE & THE PEAK DISTRICT by John N. Merrill

NOTTINGHAMSHIRE -

GHOST HUNTING AROUND NOTTINGHAMSHIRE by Rosemary Robb . ISBN 0 946404

GHOSTS & LEGENDS OF NEWARK by Rosemary Robb. ISBN 0 946404

THE GHOSTS OF WOLLATON HALL by Keith Taylor. 1SBN 0 946404

HAUNTED NOTTINGHAMSHIRE - Vol 1 - by Len Moakes . ISBN 0 946404 31 3

HAUNTED NOTTINGHAMSHIRE - Vol 2 - by Len Moakes . ISBN 0 946404 72 0

NOTTINGHAMSHIRE RAILWAY GHOSTS by John R. Smalley . ISBN 0 946404

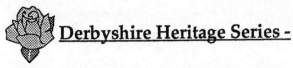 ## Derbyshire Heritage Series -

ANGLO-SAXON & VIKING DERBYSHIRE *by Richard Bunting.*

ARTISTS WITH DERBYSHIRE CONNECTIONS *by Harold Fearnehough*

BUXTON WATERS - A history of Buxton *by M.Langham & C. Wells*

THE CAPTIVE QUEEN IN DERBYSHIRE - Mary Queen of Scots - *by E.Eisenberg*

CASTLE & MANORS IN AND AROUND DERBYSHIRE *by Mike Smith*

CELTIC DERBYSHIRE *by Peter J. Naylor*

CHURCHES OF DERBYSHIRE *by John J. Anderson* .

DERBY CHINA THROUGH THREE CENTURIES *by Myra Challand*

DERBY CITY STREET TO STREET GUIDE

DERBYSHIRE CHARACTERS FOR YOUNG PEOPLE *by E. Eisenberg*

DERBYSHIRE CHURCHYARDS *by Joyce Critchlow* .

DERBYSHIRE'S MONASTIC HERITAGE *by Michael Smith*

DERBYSHIRE NOTEBOOK - *illustrated by E. Kazimierczuk*

DERBYSHIRE SUPERLATIVES *by Julie Bunting*

THE DERBYSHIRE YEAR - Customs through the years - *by E. Eisenberg*

EYAM, THE PLAGUE AND AN 1858 RAMBLE *by Clarence Daniel*

FLORENCE NIGHTINGALE *by Norma Keen*

FROM THE CRADLE TO THE GRAVE *by E. Eisenberg*

GAZETTER OF THE WHITE PEAK *by Les Robson*

GRANDFATHER THOMAS JACKSON'S RECIPES *by Thomas Jackson*

MANORS & FAMILIES OF DERBYSHIRE *Vol 1 (A - L)*

MANORS & FAMILIES OF DERBYSHIRE *Vol 2 (M - Z)*

MAY THE LORD HAVE MERCY ON YOUR SOUL *by Phillip Taylor*

NOTABLE DERBYSHIRE FAMILIES - family history - *by Roy Christian*

THE OWNERS OF MELBOURNE HALL *by Howard Usher*

THE PEAKLAND ABeCeDARY *by Jule Bunting*

PEAKLAND CHRONOLOGY *by Julie Bunting*

PREHISTORIC DERBYSHIRE *by Gerda & John Pickin*

RIVERS OF DERBYSHIRE *by Harold Fearnehough*

ROMAN DERBYSHIRE *by John Anderson*

STUART DERBYSHIRE *by Joy Childs*

SWARKESTONE BRIDGE & THE STANTON CAUSEWAY *by G.R. Heath*

THIS COSTLY COUNTESS - Bess of Hardwick - *by E. Eisenberg*

TUDOR DERBYSHIRE *by Joy Childs*

WALK THROUGH DERBY - *facsimile first published in 1827*

THE WATER CURE *by Alan Bower*

WOMEN OF DERBYSHIRE *by Susan Watson*

WORK & PLAY - Derbyshire, a photographic record - *by Alan Bower*

WRITERS WITH DERBYSHIRE CONNECTIONS *by Jane Darrall*

SPAGHETTI & BARBED WIRE - True World War 11 escapes story -
by Jack E. Fox

DERBYSHIRE GRAVES - 100 true and unusual graves - *by Peter Naylor*

ON THIS DAY....IN DERBYSHIRE - events that happened throughout the
year - *by John E. Heath*

THE EARLS AND DUKES OF DEVONSHIRE *by Julie Bunting*

TIMMY GLASS WAISTCOAT - Early 20th century life in Clay Cross
recalled - *by Jack E. Fox*

COAL, CHOCOLATE & CHIPS - 1940's and 50's life in Ripley -
by Aileen Howard.

Nottinghamshire Heritage Series -

BELL TALES by Stan Smith
.......ISBN 0 946404

THE CIVIL WAR IN THE TRENT VALLEY
by Andrew Polkey ....ISBN 0 946404

FOR CONSPICUOUS GALLANTRY
- Local V.C. Holders - by N. McCrery ......ISBN. 0 946404

HISTORY OF SUTTON IN ASHFIELD
- facsimile of 1907 edition .....ISBN 0 946404

LORD BYRON by E. Eisenberg
" Mad, bad and dangerous to know."........ISBN 0 946404 46 1

NOTTINGHAMSHIRE STRET TO STREET GUIDE .
...ISBN 0 946404

THE OLD NORTH ROAD by Joan Board
.........ISBN 0 946404.

WOLLATON HALL by Elizabeth May
Wollaton as a family home and Natural History Museum..........ISBN 0 946404

For a full list of titles - more than 250 - please write
to John Merrill at -
Footprint Press Ltd.,
19, Moseley Street,
Ripley,
Derbyshire. DE5 3DA